T H E
ARABIAN
HORSE

by Gail B. Stewart

Illustrated with photographs
by William Muñoz

Reading consultant:

John Manning, Professor of Reading
University of Minnesota

Capstone Press
MINNEAPOLIS

Capstone Press • 2440 Fernbrook Lane • Minneapolis, MN 55447

Editorial Director   John Coughlan
Managing Editor   John Martin
Copy Editor   Gil Chandler

Library of Congress Cataloging-in-Publication Data

Stewart, Gail, 1949-
    The Arabian horse / Gail B. Stewart.
        p. cm.
    Includes bibliographical references and index.
    ISBN 1-56065-244-6
    1. Arabian horse--Juvenile literature. [1. Arabian horse.
    2. Horses.]   I. Title.
SF293.A8S74   1995
636.1'12--dc20   94-29981
                                              CIP
                                              AC

ISBN: 1-56065-244-6

99 98 97 96 95 94   8 7 6 5 4 3 2 1

Table of Contents

Quick Facts about the Arabian Horse

Description

Height:	14.1 to 15.1 **hands** (equal to four-inch [ten-centimeter] segments) from the top of the shoulders. That works out to between 57 and 61 inches (140 and 150 centimeters) tall.
Weight:	850 to 1,000 lbs. (390 to 454 kilograms).
Physical features:	dense bones, **dished face**, large nostrils, small pointed ears, long flowing mane and tail, large windpipe.
Colors:	gray, brown, white, **chestnut**, **bay**.

Development

History of breed:	the oldest breed of horse on earth–well over 5,000 years old.
Place of origin:	the Arabian desert of the Middle East.
Current habitat:	many nations throughout the world, but especially in the United States, Canada, England, Saudi Arabia, Egypt, and Poland.

Food

Hay, grasses such as **timothy** and **clover**, grain
(especially oats and bran), and plenty of water. Every
day an Arabian horse needs about 14 pounds
(6 kilograms) of hay and grasses, between 4 and 12
quarts (3.8 and 11.3 liters) of oats and **bran**, and 12
gallons (45.5 liters) of water.

Life History

Life span: a well-cared-for Arabian may live
                    from 20 to 30 years.

Reproductive life: stallions are bred when they are about
                    two years old; mares when they are
                    three or four. Arabian mares carry
                    their **foals** for 11 months before
                    giving birth.

Uses

Arabians are used for breeding (strengthening and
improving other breeds of horses) and in competitions,
such as trail-riding, **halter competitions**, and racing.
Many Arabians are enjoyed for pleasure riding, too.

Chapter 1
The Perfect Horse?

According to legend, the prophet Mohammed once locked up 100 horses for seven days. The horses could not drink, even though the desert sun made them hot and thirsty.

Mohammed finally freed the horses. As they were running towards a stream to drink, he had his bugler sound a battle call. Most of the horses kept running. But five **mares** (female horses) turned towards the bugler.

Mohammed chose these horses to start a new breed–the Arabian horse.

It is easy to see why ancient people admired Arabian horses. These animals have a proud look and a graceful manner. They are quick

and strong. Many people feel that the Arabian
is the "perfect" horse.

   How did a horse from the deserts of the
Middle East become so famous around the
world? The answer lies in a long and fascinating
history. This is the story of the Arabian horse.

Chapter 2
Early Arabians

Mohammed's five mares may have been the first Arabians. No one knows exactly how the Arabian breed began. But we do know certain facts about the early Arabians.

Desert War Horses

The Arabian breed is more than 5,000 years old. It is the world's oldest breed. Arabians come from the dry, hot part of the world known as Arabia, which is part of the Middle East.

For thousands of years, people in Arabia depended on horses. The Arabs fought their wars on horseback. Riders would rush at each

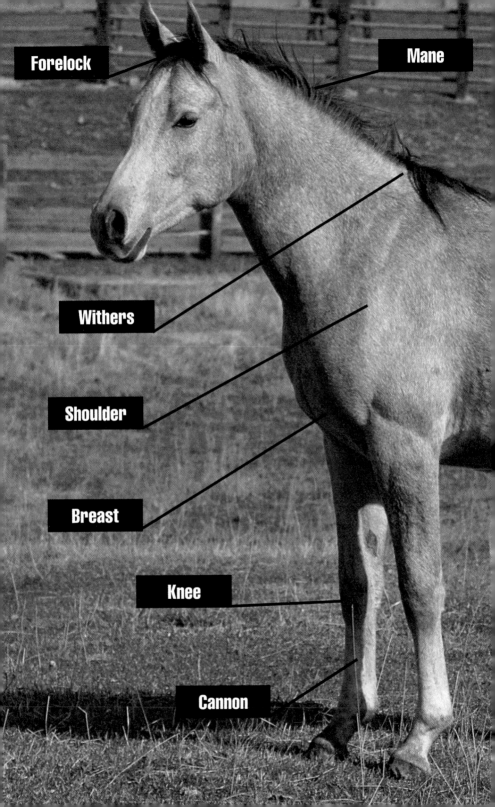

Forelock

Mane

Withers

Shoulder

Breast

Knee

Cannon

Loins

Flank

Hindquarters

Fetlock

other with swords and try to knock each other to the ground. If a man fell from his horse, he could easily be killed. That's why the armies with the best horses were the most successful.

Arabian horses were fast and strong. They could run for long distances without tiring. They could also survive for a long time with little food or water.

Living in Tents

Arabian horses made good guardians for nomadic people living in the desert. Many of these people kept their horses with them inside their tents. If a stranger or an enemy approached the tent, the horses would stamp their feet or whinny. They saved many lives this way.

Their owners treated the Arabian horses very well. When they came to an **oasis** (a desert spring), they allowed the horse to drink

first. And when a mare was ready to deliver her **foal** (baby horse), family members moved out of the tent. They did this so that the horse and her foal would have plenty of room.

Breeding Arabians Long Ago

The Arabs were careful horse breeders. They knew that certain **stallions** (male horses) and mares (female horses) produced better

foals. Over time, the Arabs learned how to mate
their horses in order to improve the breed's size,
speed, and personality.

A horse's **pedigree**–its family tree–was very important. Owners would write down the pedigree and put it in a little leather bag around the horse's neck. Sometimes they would put a charm in the bag to protect the horse from harm.

Arabians Around the World

As the years went by, the Arab peoples moved into Africa, throughout the Middle East, and into Europe. Wherever they went, people admired the flowing manes and lightning speed of the Arabian horses. It seemed these horses could run and run and never get tired.

But when people asked to buy the horses, the Arabs would usually refuse. They had a saying: "Only a fool would sell his horse, but to give one as a gift was the act of a prince."

Some Arabs sold or gave away their stallions, but never their mares. Mares were much too valuable. They were loyal and less noisy than stallions. (Soldiers trying to hide from the enemy didn't want noisy horses to give away their positions.)

Those who were lucky enough to get an Arabian used the horse for breeding. They found that mating an Arabian stallion with

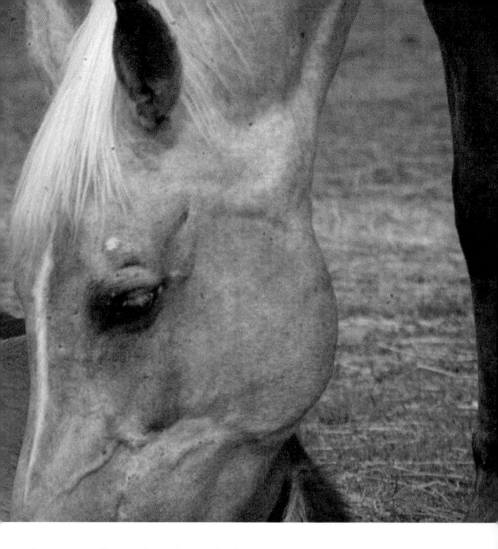

horses of another breed almost always
improved that breed, whatever it was.

Chapter 3

The Arabian Horse at Risk

Eventually, people all over the world were buying Arabian horses. When their owners used them for breeding, the result was always the same. The Arabians improved the other types of horses.

Some horse experts bred only Arabian horses. They wanted to make sure that there would always be a "pure" Arabian horse. In Poland, for example, the military wanted to use Arabians–and only Arabians–as war horses.

The Polish cavalry valued the horse's speed and endurance, just as the Arabs had.

Trouble for the Arabian

There have been bad times for the Arabian horse. Many countries have suffered wars and **turmoil**. Violence makes life uncertain and unsafe for horses as well as for people. Arabian horses were valued in Poland and Egypt, for example, but in these nations the horses also lived in danger.

Enemies would often attack horses as well as soldiers. The Polish army relied on its horses, so Poland's enemies tried to kill the Polish Arabians.

Life in wartime sometimes became so hard that people could no longer care for the horses. Many Arabians died from neglect.

Saving the Arabian

At the end of the 19th century, an English couple named Wilfrid and Anne Blunt went to Egypt to save Arabian horses in danger. The king of Egypt had died, and the Blunts feared

that the king's horses would also die. If that happened, they worried that the **purebred** Arabians of Egypt would become extinct. So they traveled to Egypt and brought some of the king's beautiful Arabians back to England.

The Blunts took the Arabians to their home in Crabbet Park, England. They called these horses "Crabbet Arabians," and devoted the rest of their lives to keeping the breed alive.

Crabbet Arabians are still valued around the world. Many people believe, as the Blunts did, that these horses are just like Arabians of ancient times.

Too Popular

Saving the Arabian from violence or neglect has not solved all of its problems. In fact, being too popular can be just as dangerous!

Books about Arabian horses, such as *The Black Stallion* by Walter Farley, made Arabian horses popular. So did movies about them. People enjoyed the spirit and energy of the horse, as well as its speed and good looks. Even people who knew very little about horses wanted to own an Arabian.

This popularity made the pure Arabian very expensive. Some horses cost millions of dollars! People who already owned fast sports cars and beautiful jewelry now wanted their own Arabians. Horse-breeding farms, hoping to make a lot of money, bred and sold Arabians.

The breeders mated too many horses, and the result was overbreeding. Sometimes the breeders were not careful about the stallions and mares they used. Many foals had parents with more weaknesses than strengths.

Cruel Training

Some people even tried to make Arabians nervous and bad-tempered. They felt this made the breed more exciting. They used whips or loud noises to frighten the horses. They also trained the animals to stamp their feet and snort during horse shows.

This was cruel, and it didn't help the breed. The breeders and trainers simply were trying to make money. They didn't really care about the horses. This kind of training gave purebred Arabians a character different than that of the Arabians of long ago.

Solving the Arabian's Problems

In recent years, things have been improving for the Arabians. People have learned that breeding Arabians is not an easy way to get rich. Changing the horse's personality is also a bad idea. Horse-show judges don't like owners to use whips. An Arabian who acts frightened and nervous in a competition probably won't win.

"I think things have really changed in the last five years," says one Arabian horse owner. "I see more owners and breeders who care about their horses. The Arabian is simply too magnificent an animal to ruin by overbreeding and poor training."

Chapter 4

The Arabian
Horse Today

The Arabian horse is bred in the United States, England, Canada, Spain, Saudi Arabia, and many other countries. Even though the breed began in the hot Arabian desert, the modern Arabian is at home almost anywhere in the world.

Physical Traits of the Arabian

Arabians in different places may have different features. Some breeders prefer faster horses. Others breed for a certain size or color.

Even so, all Arabians share some characteristics.

Arabians are small compared to other breeds. Everywhere in the world, horses are measured in **hands** (four-inch [10-centimeter] sections). From the **withers** (the top of a horse's shoulders) to the ground, Arabians measure between 14 hands, 1 inch (14 hands, 2.5 centimeters) and 15 hands, 1 inch (15 hands, 2.5 centimeters).

Many breeds stand taller. But there are none more exciting to look at. Arabians have a proud look, as if they knew how beautiful they are. They have small, pointed ears and large eyes. Their tails and manes are silky and long.

An Arabian has what is called a **dished face**, meaning one that curves inward just below the eyes. Its nostrils are large, but its lips and muzzle are very small. Some Arabian experts say the horse looks as though it could sip tea from a teacup.

Some of the Arabian's features lie below the surface. The Arabian, for instance, has

stronger bones than many other horses. This allows the Arabian to carry more weight than horses with lighter bones.

The Arabian's endurance comes partly from its large windpipe. This allows the horse to get a lot of oxygen into its lungs with every breath. Arabians don't tire as quickly as horses with smaller breathing systems.

A Horse of Many Colors

All horses have a layer of skin and a thin coat of hair. Many breeds have skin that is pinkish or spotted with dark blotches. But the Arabian has a skin of pure black. Experts say that this color comes from the horse's origins in the desert. Black skin protected the early Arabians from the hot sun.

The color of the coat above the skin is almost never black. The desert Arabs took care never to breed horses with a black coat. They knew that such a coat would absorb the heat from the sun, making the horse hot and tired.

The Arabs had strong opinions about the colors of their horses. They thought that spotted horses looked like pigs or cows. If a spotted horse was born, it would not be bred. Nor were **palominos**–horses with a golden coat and white mane and tail. Palominos were considered bad luck for the entire camp.

There are many colors of Arabians: gray, brown, white, **chestnut** (reddish), and **bay** (reddish with black legs, mane, or tail). Many Arabians are born with dark coats that get lighter as they get older.

35

Chapter 5
Arabians in Action

The days of wars fought on horseback are long gone. But Arabians still have the features that made them so important to the Arabs long ago.

A Running Horse

Some people who own Arabians use them just for pleasure riding. It's fun to own a horse that loves to run. And running is what Arabians do best.

Arabians also compete in different kinds of shows. **Halter competitions** are like beauty contests. Experts judge each horse as the

owner leads it around a ring. Prizes are given
for the best-looking horses.

Arabians are also a popular racing horse. In
the United States, most horse races are for
Thoroughbreds, but many other nations race
only Arabians. In Poland, Egypt, Greece,
Spain, and other countries, Arabian races are
sometimes three kilometers (about two miles)
long.

One of the most exciting competitions for Arabians is a trail-riding contest. Their endurance and strength make Arabians good at such contests. They almost always win.

In a trail-riding competition, horse and rider try to complete a course before the other contestants. It's tougher than it sounds!

The courses are sometimes 100 miles (160 kilometers) long, and the trails are very difficult. Horses and riders must cross winding rivers and climb steep hills. Speed is important, but along most of the course the horses can only walk or trot.

Trail-riding courses are hard on horses. Contestants must stop along the way so that veterinarians can make sure the horses are healthy. A 100-mile (160-kilometer) trail ride can take 24 hours to complete.

A Horse With a Proud History

A warrior who depended on his mare in the desert sometimes called her *Banat er Rih*, which means "daughter of the wind" in Arabic.

It is easy to tell that modern Arabian horses still have a little of that desert history in them.

"I love to watch these horses when they run," says an Arabian breeder. "They tear over the ground just for the pure joy of it. Even if there is no rider, they run with their heads stretched out and their manes flying. It isn't hard to imagine ancient warriors on their backs. No other animal makes me feel as **awestruck** as an Arabian."

The Arabian, with its 5,000-year history, is as exciting today as it was in years gone by.

Glossary

awestruck–to be amazed by something

bay–a reddish-brown horse with black legs, mane, and tail

bran–grain used as horse feed

chestnut–a reddish brown horse with no black markings

clover–a flowering herb that horses feed on

dished face–one that curves inward under the eyes. This is visible in the profile of the horse.

foal–a young horse

halter competition–a beauty contest for horses

hands–four-inch (10-centimeter) segments used to measure a horse

mare–a female horse

oasis–a desert spring with fresh water and sometimes vegetation and shelter

palomino–a golden horse with a silvery-white mane and tail

pedigree–a list of a horse's ancestors

purebred–a horse whose ancestors all belong to the same breed

stallion–a male horse

Thoroughbred–a breed of racing horse that was bred in England

timothy–a rough grass that horses eat

turmoil–confusing disturbance

withers–the top of a horse's shoulders

To Learn More

Balch, Glenn. *The Book of Horses*. New York: Four Winds, 1967.

Brown, Fern G. *Horses and Foals*. New York: Franklin Watts, 1986.

Clutton-Brock, Juliet. *Horse* (Eyewitness Books). New York: Alfred A. Knopf, 1992.

Henry, Marguerite. *All About Horses*. New York: Random House, 1962.

Patent, Dorothy Hinshaw. *Arabian Horses*. New York: Holiday House, 1982.

You can read articles about Arabian horses in *The Arabian Horse Times*, *Horse Illustrated*, and *Horse and Rider*.

Some Useful Addresses

Arabian Horse Registry of America
12000 Zuni St.
Westminster, CO 80234

International Arabian Horse Association
P.O. Box 33696
Denver, CO 80233

Arabian Horse Owners Foundation
4633 E. Broadway, Suite 131
Tucson, AZ 85711

Arabian Horse Museum
Box 3030
Barnes, MD 20703

Canadian Arabian Horse Registry
R.R. 1
Bowden, AB T0M 0K0 CANADA

World Arabian Horse Organization
Capital House, 11 Waterfront Quay
Manchester M5 2XW, England

Index